The
Lark Rise
Cook's
Note Book

———— ✗ ————

THE
LARK RISE
COOK'S
NOTE BOOK

MARY NORWAK

CENTURY

LONDON MELBOURNE AUCKLAND JOHANNESBURG

First published in 1986 for Marks & Spencer p.l.c. by
Century Benham Ltd
62-65 Chandos Place, London WC2N 4NW

This edition published in 1987 by
Century Hutchinson Ltd,
Brookmount House,
62-65 Chandos Place, Covent Garden, London WC2N 4NW

Century Hutchinson Publishing Group (Australia) Pty Ltd
16-22 Church Street, Hawthorn, Melbourne, Victoria 3122, Australia

Century Hutchinson Group (NZ) Ltd
32-34 View Road, PO Box 40-086, Glenfield, Auckland 10, New Zealand

Century Hutchinson Group (SA) Pty Ltd
PO Box 337, Bergvlei 2012, South Africa

Edited, designed and produced by
Shuckburgh Reynolds Ltd, 289 Westbourne Grove, London W11 2QA

ISBN 0 7126 1763 9

Design by Behram Kapadia
Woodcut engravings by Thomas Bewick
Typeset by SX Composing Ltd, Rayleigh, Essex
Printed in Spain

Contents

Introduction

The earliest recipes are traditionally handed down verbally, for until the nineteenth century there were few printed cookery books and few cooks who could read them. Mothers taught their daughters and mistresses their servants and the young unskilled cook had to watch carefully, memorize ingredients and methods. Ingredients could not be measured accurately nor fires controlled and nobody understood the scientific reasons for culinary processes. Thus there arose the "little bit of this and little bit of that" type of recipe and results could not be guaranteed when the cook had only learned to "bake till done".

In a few households, however, women who could read and write took great pleasure in recording their favourite dishes and it became a pleasant custom to collect recipes from friends and members of the family. A recipe would be identified by the name of the giver, sometimes a date and even a comment on whether it worked satisfactorily and tasted good. These books were often known as commonplace books and were also used to note tradesmen's addresses, medical prescriptions and even lines of poetry. The books became treasured family possessions, handed on to daughters as they in turn took over the management of households.

Now that newspapers and magazines print so many recipes most of us have a huge collection of clippings in the kitchen drawer, but it is much more practical and attractive to return to the tradition of keeping a note book. This Note Book is divided into chapters, similar to those in the Recipe Book. At the beginning of each chapter a few recipes have been given, then the pages have been left blank for you to complete with your own carefully chosen favourites.

It is a mistake, though, to record every recipe that takes your fancy. The book should be for those special dishes which the family ask for again and again, the birthday chicken dish, the children's favourite chocolate cake and Mother's special way with an apple pie. Here, too, is a place for those seasonal recipes, rarely used but absolutely vital to the success of a family occasion – Granny's Christmas Pudding or Father's Mulled Wine. Some cooks like to make extra notes on the recipes indicating substitute ingredients or whether extra seasoning is required or suitable accompaniments. To make the book a real treasure for daughters and grandchildren, it's delightful to record the names of the recipe givers or their houses so that future generations can know that they are working with a very special Cook's Note Book.

Starters

Potted Shrimps

4 oz BUTTER
1 lb PEELED PINK OR BROWN SHRIMPS
½ TEASPOON GROUND NUTMEG
½ TEASPOON GROUND MACE
PINCH OF CAYENNE PEPPER
4 oz CLARIFIED BUTTER

1 · Melt the butter over low heat and add the shrimps and spices. Stir well over low heat so that the shrimps are completely covered in butter.
2 · Place in a serving dish (or individual dishes), making sure that all the butter and spices are included with the shrimps. Leave for 15 minutes until cool and almost set.
3 · Melt the clarified butter and pour over the shrimps. Leave in a cool place until firm and set.

Potted Pork

2 lb BELLY PORK
4 oz LARD
SALT AND PEPPER
PINCH OF GROUND NUTMEG

The meat should be weighed when bones and skin have been removed, and it is necessary to use about 3 lb meat to get the required amount.

1 · Cut the meat into 1 in. cubes.
2 · Put into a thick saucepan with the lard and ¼ pint cold water. Cover and simmer over very low heat for 4 hours, or cook in a very low oven (275°F/140°C/Gas Mark 1).
3 · Drain thoroughly and keep the liquid.
4 · Use two forks to pull apart the meat and fat so that it is shredded finely. Season well with salt, pepper and nutmeg, and put into small pots.
5 · Pour on the reserved liquid. Cool and cover with foil or lids.
6 · Store in the refrigerator, where the mixture will keep for up to 2 months. Serve spread on bread or toast.

Liver and Bacon Loaf

6 STREAKY BACON RASHERS
8 oz PIG'S LIVER
8 oz FAT BACON
1 LARGE ONION
1 GARLIC CLOVE
3 oz BUTTER
SALT AND PEPPER
1 oz PLAIN FLOUR
½ PINT MILK
PINCH OF GROUND NUTMEG
3 BAY LEAVES

1 · Remove rinds from bacon and press the rashers out with a knife.

2 · Line a loaf tin with the rashers.

3 · Chop the liver, bacon, onion and garlic and fry in 2 oz butter for 5 minutes, stirring well.

4 · Mince finely or chop finely in a food processor, and season well with salt and pepper.

5 · Melt the remaining butter and work in the flour. Add the milk and stir well over low heat until the sauce is thick. Season with nutmeg.

6 · Blend the liver mixture and sauce well and place in the prepared tin.

7 · Top with bay leaves.

8 · Cover with foil and put into a roasting tin containing 1 in. hot water. Bake in a moderate oven (350°F/180°C/Gas Mark 4) for 1 hour.

9 · Cool under weights for 24 hours before serving with toast or salad.

Vermouth Prawns

1/2 lb Cooked Prawns.
2 cloves Garlic Chopped.
3-4 Parsley Sprigs.
1/2 cup Olive Oil.
1/2 Cup dry Vermouth
2 Tablesp. Wine Vinegar.
1/2 Teasp. dried Tarragon.
1 Teasp. Sugar.
Dash Cayenne Pepper.
1 Teasp. Salt.

Place Prawns in a bowl. Combine Prawns c remaining ingredients Cover a chill overnight. Stirring nor a again. Serves 10.

Maria's Minestroni

1 Piece of Pumkin or White Turnip.
1 Courgette
Peas
Green Beans.
1 Potatoe
1 Teaspoon Basil.
Crushed Garlic.
Oil.
Boil well in Water. When cooked liquidise Add Pasta Season with Salt a Pepper to Taste.

Maria's Moroccan Soup.

½ lb. Lentils.   ⎱ Soak
½ lb. Chick Peas.   ⎰ Overnight.

Tomatoe (Large).
Potatoe
Celery
½ lb. Beef Lean.
Water
Boil well. Liquidise when cooked.

Chunky Tomato Soup

Onions chopped.
Carrots ¼" dice ,
Celery Sticks ¼" dice .
Fl. Oz Olive Oil ,
Unsalted Butter
Bay Leaf .
Large Garlic Clove .
Smoked Bacon Rinded &
cut into strips
lb Ripe Tomatoes pref Plum .
1½ O Chicken Stock
well Bunch Fresh Basil
   "   " Tarragon
Tomato Puree to Taste .

Sweat Veg in Oil & Butter for a few minutes t
ditto Add Bay Leaf & Garlic. Add the Bacon continue
to cook for 5 mins
Cut Tomatoes into 8 pieces Add to Veg Cover pan
& cook gently for 15 mins   Stir mixture
occasionally   When Tomatoes have softened
Add Stock. Leave to cook for further
20 mins. Add chopped herbs . Season &
Salt & Pepper Add a little Puree

Main Meals

Roast Pork with Sage Stuffing

1 LEG OR LOIN OF PORK
SALT AND PEPPER
OIL
2 LARGE ONIONS
3 oz BUTTER
2 oz FRESH WHITE BREADCRUMBS
2 TEASPOONS CHOPPED FRESH SAGE

1 · Score the skin of the pork with a sharp knife and rub in a little oil, then sprinkle with salt and pepper. This gives a crisp crackling when the meat is cooked.
2 · Roast in a moderately hot oven (375°F/190°C/Gas Mark 5) for 30 minutes per lb.
3 · The stuffing may be put into a boned joint or cooked separately in the same oven. Chop the onions coarsely and simmer until soft in just enough water to cover them. Add breadcrumbs, butter, sage and plenty of seasoning, and mix well.
4 · To cook separately, put into a greased ovenware dish and dot with butter, and cook for 1 hour with the joint.
5 · Serve with apple sauce.

Sage Sausages

2 lb PORK
1 TABLESPOON FRESH SAGE
4 oz FRESH BREADCRUMBS
SALT AND PEPPER

1 · The pork should be a mixture of equal fat and lean. Mince the meat very finely or chop in a food processor.
2 · Put the sage leaves into a bowl and cover with boiling water. Drain off the water and chop or mince the leaves finely.
3 · Add to the meat with the breadcrumbs and season with salt and pepper.
4 · Fill the mixture into skins or form into small round cakes.

Pot-Roast Chicken

3½-4 lb CHICKEN
1½ oz BUTTER
2 CELERY STICKS
6 SMALL ONIONS
2 MEDIUM CARROTS
1 SMALL TURNIP
½ PINT CHICKEN STOCK OR WATER
SALT AND PEPPER
1 TABLESPOON CHOPPED FRESH PARSLEY

1 · Melt the butter and brown the chicken lightly in a thick pan.
2 · Slice the celery, onions, carrots and turnip thinly. Add to the chicken with the stock or water, salt and pepper.
3 · Cover and simmer for 2 hours, basting occasionally with the liquid.

4 · Sprinkle with parsley just before serving.
5 · If preferred, the chicken may be cooked in a moderate oven (350°F/180°C/Gas Mark 4).

Lamb and Caper Sauce

1 LEG OR SHOULDER OF LAMB
1 TEASPOON SALT
2 oz PEARL BARLEY
1 LARGE ONION
8 oz CARROTS
8 oz TURNIPS
SPRIG OF PARSLEY
SPRIG OF THYME
1 BAY LEAF
1 oz BUTTER
1 oz PLAIN FLOUR
3 TABLESPOONS CAPERS

1 · Weigh the meat and calculate the cooking time at 25 minutes per lb.
2 · Put into a large thick pan and add the salt. Cover with water and leave to simmer for 1 hour.
3 · Slice the onion, carrots and turnips and add to the liquid with the herbs. Cover and continue simmering gently for the rest of the cooking time.

4 · Just before serving, melt the butter and work in the flour. Add 1 pint cooking liquid gradually, and stir over low heat until smooth and creamy. Stir in the capers and season to taste.
5 · Arrange the lamb and vegetables on a serving dish and serve the sauce separately.

Beef Teriyaki 1½ lbs tender steak 3 Tablesps. Oil
1 clove garlic 1 large Onion (Rings) 1 large Red 2 Peppers
4 small Zucchini sliced 2 Medium sized carrots in thin stic
½ cup light Soya Sauce 1 Tablesp. Sugar ¼ cup Sweet Sher
8 ozs thin egg noodles 8 ozs mushrooms

Rx cut steak into paperthin slices Heat oil é garli
Remove garlic add meat few pieces at a time a brown
quickly. Remove from pan. Add Onion Rings cook 2 min
Add Peppers Zucchini a carrots Cook 2 mins stir frying
Add soy sauce sugar a Sherry. Cook noodles in
boiling salted water. Separate c chopsticks Drain whe
just tender Return meat to pan, mix in mushrooms
a noodles a cook 2-3 mins. Serves 6.

Indonesian Meatballs c Rice

2 oz Butter
1 small onion finely chopped.
1 Teasp. ground Cummin
1 " " Coriander.
½ " " Allspice
½ " " Ginger
2 " Cornflour.
1 Egg beaten.
1 lb Beef or Pork minced
salt a Pepper.

Serves 4

2 ozs butter.
4 cups boiled Rice (1½ cups Ra
3 small peppers Red Green a
yellow,
1 Can Mandarins.
Heat butter in pan add onion
until soft. Add spices a cook
for 1 min. stirring. Allow to
cool then mix c Remaining
ingredients. Shape into ball
a fry in butter until brown all ov
approx 6 mins
Heat butter toss peppers over
Mod heat until softening Add
Rice a stir until piping hot.
Fold in Mandarins season c
salt a pepper

Serves 4.

...cken Piraeus.

Small chickens 1½ lb each
...t & Bl. Pepper.
Teasp. Cinnamon
Tablesp. Lemon juice
Tablesps. Olive Oil.
cup Orange juice.
" Chicken stock
extra Tablesp. Oil.
lb Zucchini cut into sticks
clove Garlic
Oranges peeled & sliced.

split chicken in ½ rub č salt pepper cinnamon & lemon juice Cover & allow to stand ½ hr. Heat oil in deep frying pan brown chicken all sides. Add Orange juice & stock Cover & simmer until chicken is almost tender (25 mins) Fry Zucchini quickly in oil Season č salt & pepper. Add to bird č Orange simmer approx 5 mins. Remove from pan & Reduce liquid spoon over chicken Serve č boiled Rice.

...uffed Chicken fillets in Marsala

hicken ½ Breasts.
...in seasoned flour.
hin slices of Ham.
hin slices Swiss Cheese.
...oked Asparagus Spears.
...g Butter
up Marsala Wine
up Chicken Stock
...ely chopped shallots
...ing to get brown from pan,
...mmer until reduced a little
...ie & string, arrange on a heated
...e, spoon sauce over
...mkle finely chopped shallots over
...rves 6 - 8.

Place fillets between sheets of cling film & flatten out with a Rolling Pin Dip in seasoned flour & shake off excess Place a slice of Ham then a slice of Cheese on each fillet & Asparagus Spear in the middle. Roll the fillets up neatly, tucking in the ends & tie in place č string. Heat Butter in a large heavy frying pan & slowly brown on all sides This will take 6-8 minutes. Remove Rolls & keep warm Add Marsala & stock to the pan. Bring to the boi...

Horseradish Beef c̄ Golden Topping

2 lb Beef.
Plain flour seasoned.
2 Tablesp. Oil
2 Large Onions sliced
Salt & pepper.
½ Teasp. Thyme (dried)
¾ cup Tomatoe Puree.
¾ Cup. Water.
2 Teasp. Horseradish sauce

Topping.
1½ lbs swede Turnips
4 Large Carrots
1 Medium Onion
Salt & pepper.
Good pinch Nutmeg.
3 Teasp. Brown Sugar.
1 oz Butter.

Cut steak into 1 inch pieces
Coat c̄ seasoned flour.
Heat oil & brown meat all over.
Drain & place in casserole
Add Onion slices to pan & soften
Add salt, pepper, thyme, Tomato puree
& water stir until boiling.
Pour over meat Cover dish &
cook in moderate oven for 2 hrs
Stir in Horseradish

Place puree on top. Dot
c̄ small pieces of butter &
Return to oven until piping

Puree   Place Veg in saucepan c̄ enough
salted water to cover. Boil until tender drain
& puree in blender. Beat in Remaining
ingredients.

Baked Veal Parcels

12 Thin slices Veal. Salt & Pepper. 2 g Bu...
1 Tablesp. Olive Oil, 1 Large Onion finely ch...
2½ cups fresh breadcrumbs. ½ cup grate...
cheese. 1 Tablesp. chopped fresh marjora...
or 1 Teasp dried. ½ cup sultanas ½ c...
chopped walnuts. 1 cup Tomato puree.
1½ cups Beef stock. 2 Teasp. Sugar.

Beat steaks c̄ a rolling pin until very th...
Season c̄ Salt & pepper. Heat oil & butt...
& fry onion until soft & golden. Mix in
breadcrumbs, cheese, marjoram, sultan...
& walnuts, season to taste. Divide
stuffing between steaks, roll up firmly, tu...
in ends. Arrange seam side down, cl...
together in a shallow dish. Heat toma...
puree c̄ stock & sugar, pour over the...
& cover tightly. Bake in Moderate ov...
180° C. for 45 minutes until veal is ten...
Serve c̄ Rice or buttered noodle...

Serves 6.

Serves 4.

Tarragon Veal Fricassee

1 lb. stewing veal
seasoned flour.
¾g Butter
large Onion finely chopped.
Tablesp. fresh Tarragon
2 Teasp. dried "
cup Sour Cream.
cup Cream.
Tablesp. lemon juice
chopped parsley to garnish.

Cut meat into bite sized pieces.
Roll in seasoned flour
Melt butter in pan & toss until
pale gold. Add onion, stock
Tarragon, bring to boil.
lower heat, cover pan &
simmer until veal is tender.
about 40 mins. Stir in Cream,
Sour cream & lemon juice &
bring to simmer. Taste for
seasoning, sprinkle & chopped
parsley.

Alisons Devilled Chicken

1 Teaspoon Ginger
1   "   "   Sugar.
1   "   "   Salt.
1   "   "   Dry Mustard
3   "   "   Curry Powder.

} Mix
Together.

2 Tablespoons Mango Chutney
2   "   "   Tomato Sauce.
2   "   "   H.P. Sauce
2   "   "   Soya Sauce.
2   "   "   Worcestor Sauce

} Mix
ē
above.

Dash of Tobasco
Pinch of Pepper.
Spread over Chicken joints leave
to Marinade for at least 1 hr.
Wrap Chicken with Marinade
in Tinfoil Cook in Oven.

Marias Stuffed Courgettes

½ Courgettes. Boil in Salted Water.
when cooked Drain well.
Take Flesh out of Courgettes & mash
Add Breadcrumbs, Grated Cheese,
Marjoram, Parsley, & Beaten Eggs
Salt & Pepper. Fill Courgette Shells &
Bake in Oven.

Maria's Chicken

Fry Chicken joints in Olive Oil.
" Garlic
when browned Add 1 Tablespoon. Almonds. Pour White Wine over
chicken & continue until cooked.

Almondigas

1 lb Minced Beef.
¼ lb grated cheese.
Clove of Garlic.
Parsley
Marjoram
2 Eggs
Bread Crums.

Mix Ingredients & make Meat Balls
Roll in Flour.
Sauce   Heat a little Oil in Pan. Add fine
chopped Onion 1 Bay leaf & Saffron. Ad
1 Pint of Water bring to Boil. Add Meat Ba
Before serving (allow to cool slightly) Add 1 Be
Egg + Lemon Juice Stir in Briskly & eat.

Parsnip Croquettes

1½ lb Parsnips Peeled & cut into Chunks.
2 oz Low Fat soft cheese,
1 Egg + 1 Egg Yolk. Salt & Pepper,
4 oz Breadcrumbs.

① Cook Parsnips in B. Salted Water
until Tender Drain well, return to
Pan. Cook over high heat, stirring
until all water has evaporated
② Mash Parsnips then beat in
cheese & Egg Yolk Allow to cool
③ With Floured hands shape the
mixture into Dumpy logs about 2" long
Place on Baking Sheet & chill until firm ~ 15 mins

④ Coat Croquettes in li
beaten egg, then Breadc
& chill for further 15 m
⑤ Place the Baking S
of Croquettes under
grill & cook for abo
15 mins turning
frequently serve
garnished with Water
or Parsley.

Serves 4 as Veg. W

30

Fisherman's Pie (Serves 4).

2 lbs White Fish .   4 oz Butter
1 Pint Milk .   2 oz Plain Flour
2 oz Peeled Prawns .   2 Hard Boiled Eggs Roughly Chopped
1 Level Teaspoon Capers   3 Tablespoons Fresh Parsley .
1 Tablespoon Lemon Juice. Salt & Freshly Milled Pepper .

For the Topping
2 lbs Freshly Cooked Potatoes
2 oz Butter & 1/4 Pint Soured Cream
Freshly Grated Nutmeg .

Arrange Fish in a baking tin & season with Salt & Pepper. Pour over 1/2 Pint Milk dot c butter & bake in the Oven. 15-20 mins. Bake off & reserve cooking liquid. Remove skin & bones from Fish & break flesh into large pieces.

Make sauce by melting the remaining 3 oz Butter in a saucepan stir in flour & gradually add the fish cooking liquid, stirring well after each addition. When all liquid is in, finish off sauce by addition of remaining 1/2 pint Milk, season c Salt & Pepper. Mix the Fish c the sauce, add the Prawns, hard-boiled Eggs, capers & parsley. Stir in Lemon Juice. Pour mixture into a 3 Pint, well greased baking dish. Cream cooked Potatoes c Butter, cream & grated Nutmeg & spread evenly over Fish, on high shelf at 200 for about 1/2 hour or til heated thro' & browned.

Puddings and Desserts

Apple Roly-Poly

8 oz SELF-RAISING FLOUR
PINCH OF SALT
PINCH OF GROUND MIXED SPICE
4 oz SHREDDED SUET
2 LARGE COOKING APPLES
2 oz CURRANTS
2 oz LIGHT SOFT BROWN SUGAR
GRATED RIND OF 1 LEMON

1 · Stir the flour, salt, spice and suet together and add just enough cold water to make a firm dough.

2 · Roll out ¼ in. thick into a rectangle. Peel and core the apples and chop them finely. Sprinkle on the dough, leaving a narrow border all round.

3 · Sprinkle with currants, sugar and lemon rind.

4 · Roll up firmly and wrap in greased greaseproof paper and then in foil, sealing the edges firmly but leaving room for expansion.

5 · Put into a pan of boiling water and cover. Boil gently for 2 hours, adding a little more boiling water if necessary.

6 · Unroll carefully and serve hot with some melted apricot jam or custard.

Saucer Pancakes

2 oz BUTTER
2 oz CASTER SUGAR
2 EGGS
2 oz SELF-RAISING FLOUR
½ PINT MILK
8 TABLESPOONS JAM
A LITTLE CASTER SUGAR

1 · Set the oven to moderate heat (375°F/ 190°C/Gas Mark 5).

2 · Grease 8 old saucers and put them into the oven to heat. Cream the butter and sugar until soft and light. Beat in the eggs one at a time with a little flour. Beat in the remaining flour.

3 · Heat the milk to lukewarm and pour into the mixture. Beat well and pour into the warm saucers.

4 · Bake for 20 minutes.

5 · Put a spoonful of jam on half of each pancake. Fold over and sprinkle with a little sugar before serving hot.

✗

Lemon Cheesecake

1 LARGE LEMON
4 oz CASTER SUGAR
4 EGGS AND 2 EGG YOLKS
4 oz UNSALTED BUTTER
3 TABLESPOONS DOUBLE CREAM
6 oz SHORTCRUST PASTRY

1 · Grate the lemon rind and squeeze out the lemon juice.
2 · Put into a bowl with the sugar, eggs and egg yolks and beat together.
3 · Heat the butter gently until melted. Take off the heat and stir in the cream. Stir into the lemon mixture and beat well.
4 · Line a greased 7 in. flan tin with the pastry, prick with a fork, and bake in a moderate oven (350°F/180°C/Gas Mark 4) for 20 minutes. Cool for 10 minutes.
5 · Pour in the lemon mixture and bake in a moderately hot oven (375°F/190°C/Gas Mark 5) for 30 minutes.
6 · Serve hot or cold.

Oxford (Apricot) Pudding

6 LARGE FRESH APRICOTS
5 oz CASTER SUGAR
4 EGGS
4 TABLESPOONS DOUBLE CREAM
8 oz PUFF PASTRY

If fresh apricots are not available, the same quantity of canned ones may be used, but they should be well-drained.

1 · Steam the fresh apricots until tender.
2 · Cut up the apricots in small pieces and mix with 1 oz sugar.
3 · Leave until cold and beat in the egg yolks and cream.
4 · Line a 7 in. flan tin with pastry and pour in the apricot mixture.
5 · Bake the pudding in a hot oven (400°F/200°C/Gas Mark 6) for 15 minutes.
6 · Reduce heat to moderate (350°F/180°C/Gas Mark 4) and continue baking for 15 minutes.
7 · Whisk the egg whites to stiff peaks and fold in the remaining sugar. Spoon on top of the apricot filling and continue baking for 10 minutes.

Judy's Chocolate Rum Gateaux

1 choclate Sponge.
Soak cake in Sherry.

Filling
1 Pint of Cream Whipped stiffly.
½ lb Choclate Melt
2 ozs of ground Almonds.
2 ozs of Sugar.
3 Tablespoons of Rum.
Add all ingredients to Cream.
Put between layers of Cake &
cover cake Top & sides with
mixture

Joans Choclate Box.

¼ lb Choclate ⎤ melt   ¼ lb Digestive
¼ lb Butter ⎦ together,   Biscuits.
1½ ozs Sugar.   ½ Pint Cream.
1 Egg.
chopped Almonds ⎤ 4 ozs lined loaf Tin.
Cherries   ⎥ of each. & add some
Raisins   ⎦   Rum.
2 Hand fulls Merangues.
Beat in Sugar & Egg to Melted mixture
Mix in Nuts & Fruit & Crushed Biscuits.
Put ½ mixture into lined loaf Tin Then
add lightly broken Merangues. Add
Remainder. Leave in Fridge over
night. Turn out onto plate. Cover
with Whipped Cream. Decorate č Choc etc.

✗ My Christmas Pudding.

14 ozs. Raisins   ⎤ Soak in
14 ozs. Sultanas   ⎥ Black Rum
6 ozs Figs   ⎥ a good glass ful
6 ozs Cherries.   ⎥ cover & leave at
4 ozs Peel   ⎦ least 24 hrs.

1 grated Apple
2 grated Carrots.
5 ozs Flour
5 ozs Breadcrumbs.
8 ozs Butter
3 ozs Ground Almonds.
2 Teaspoons Mixed Spice.
5 Eggs.

Mix Apple & Carrots into fruit
chop Butter up into small pieces
& mix thro' fruit
Mix in Sugar & Ground Almond
Add Breadcrumbs & mix well
Mix Spice č flour & add
gradually with Eggs. Mix well
Make 2 Puddings approx
3 lbs each. Divide into 2 Puddi
Basins Cover. Boil each for 3 h
in Pressure Cooker. Turn out of
Pudding Basin when cold. Wrap in
Greaseproof paper 1st & then Tin Fo
Heat before Serving.

Ricotta Ice Cream

Pistachio Nuts
Pecan Nuts
Hazelnuts (toasted).
Grated Rind 1 Orange.
    "   "   1 Lemon.
Crystalized ginger.
Glacé Cherries.
Dried Apricots
Raisins
Ricotta
tablesps. Amaretto, Maraschino
    or Brandy.
teaspoon Vanilla Essence.
Egg Yolks.
Castor sugar.

Roughly chop Nuts & mix c̄
Grated Hazelnuts Citrus Rind
dig chop Ginger & cherries
Apricots & Raisins & add to
bowl.
Mix the Ricotta thro' the
fruit mixture then beat in
essence & liqueur.
Egg Yolks & sugar in a
bowl or whisk hard until very
& creamy
Ricotta mixture evenly thro'
the Egg & sugar until smooth.

Line a 7" x 5" loaf Tin c̄ a double layer of
Baking Parchment. Pour in mixture, level the top
cover c̄ , chill in FREEZER until firm — at least
overnight.
To serve. Remove from Tin, peel off paper.
Stand on a serving dish Serve in slices.

Yogurt Jelly

1 Jelly
Dissolve in ½ pt Water (boiling)
1 Carton Yogurt } mix into Jelly
Pureed Fruit } when cooled.
Serve c̄ Fruit Coulee + Cream.
            or Ice Cream.

Rhubarb Roly Poly

6 ozs Castor Sugar
Juice of 1 small Lemon.
¼ pint + 4 Tablespoons Water
1 lb Rhubarb.
3 ozs light Brown Sugar.
1 level Teaspoon ground Cinnamon.
4 ozs Seedless Raisins
8 ozs Plain Flour.
3 level Teaspoons Baking Powder
¼ level Teaspoon Salt.
1½ ozs Rolled Oats
4 ozs Margarine.
¼ pint Milk
1 oz Melted Margarine
Shallow Ovenproof Dish

Sift Flour, B. Powder, Salt.
Add Rolled Oats, then Margarine
chopped into pieces. Crumb in ē
fingers. Stir in just enough Milk
to make a soft but not sticky dough.
Turn dough onto a floured board
a Roll, not too thinly into a Large
Rectangle about 12" X 8"

＊Scatter the fruit mixture ev
over it. Roll up, using Roll
pin to keep it straight
Grease Tin. Cut the Roll into 8
even pieces & arrange on end
too tightly in the dish. Brush
surface ē melted Margarine
Pour syrup over Rolls.

Syrup
Put Castor Sugar, lemon juice
water into saucepan. Stir over
gentle heat to dissolve sugar.
Boil for 2 minutes. Leave to
＊ Mix Rhubarb, light brown Su
Cinnamon & Raisins ＊
Pour syrup over Rolls. Cook
in hot Oven 200°C. for ½ an h
Reduce heat to 180° & cook for
further 20 mins.
Can be cooked day before &
Re heated

Cakes

Cider Cake

8 oz PLAIN FLOUR
½ TEASPOON BICARBONATE OF SODA
½ TEASPOON GROUND GINGER
PINCH OF GROUND NUTMEG
4 oz BUTTER
4 oz CASTER SUGAR
2 EGGS
¼ PINT DRY CIDER

1 · Grease and base-line a 7 in. square cake tin with greased greaseproof paper.
2 · Sift together the flour, soda and spices.
3 · Cream the butter and sugar until light and fluffy.
4 · Beat in one of the eggs and half the flour mixture. Add the other egg and a little more flour.
5 · Whisk the cider until frothy and stir into the mixture.
6 · Fold in the remaining flour.
7 · Place the mixture in the tin.
8 · Bake in a moderately low oven (325°F/160°C/Gas Mark 3) for 45 minutes.
9 · Cool in the tin for 5 minutes, then turn on to a wire rack to cool.

Honey Spice Loaf

2 oz BUTTER
5 oz CLEAR HONEY
5 oz DEMERARA SUGAR
10 oz PLAIN FLOUR
1 TEASPOON BICARBONATE OF SODA
1 TEASPOON GROUND MIXED SPICE
1 TEASPOON GROUND GINGER
1 TEASPOON GROUND CINNAMON
4 oz CHOPPED MIXED CANDIED PEEL
1 EGG
¼ PINT MILK

1 · Grease and base-line a 1 lb loaf tin.
2 · Melt the butter in a large thick pan over low heat. Take off the heat and stir in the honey and sugar. Mix well and leave the mixture to cool.
3 · Sieve the flour with the soda and spices, and stir in the peel.
4 · Beat the egg and milk into the honey mixture. Pour into the flour and beat until very smooth.
5 · Pour into the tin and bake in a moderate oven (350°F/180°C/Gas Mark 4) for 1¼ hours.
6 · Cool in the tin for 5 minutes, then turn on to a wire rack to cool.
7 · Serve sliced with butter.

Rock Cakes

2 oz PLAIN FLOUR
1 TEASPOON BAKING POWDER
PINCH OF SALT
6 oz BUTTER
6 oz GRANULATED SUGAR
3 oz CURRANTS
1½ oz CHOPPED MIXED CANDIED PEEL
¼ TEASPOON GROUND MIXED SPICE
¼ TEASPOON GROUND NUTMEG
1 EGG
3 TABLESPOONS MILK

1 · Grease a baking sheet and then flour it lightly.

2 · Sieve the flour, baking powder and salt together and rub in the butter until the mixture is like fine breadcrumbs.

3 · Stir in the sugar, currants, peel and spices.

4 · Beat the egg and stir into the mixture with the milk to give a stiff consistency.

5 · Put rocky heaps of the mixture on to the baking sheet and bake in a moderate oven (375°F/190°C/Gas Mark 5) for 15 minutes.

6 · Cool on a wire rack.

Special Seed Cake

8 oz SELF-RAISING FLOUR
PINCH OF SALT
PINCH OF GROUND NUTMEG
1 TEASPOON CARAWAY SEEDS
8 oz BUTTER
8 oz CASTER SUGAR
5 EGGS
3 oz CHOPPED CANDIED ORANGE PEEL
2 TABLESPOONS BRANDY
Topping
2 TEASPOONS CASTER SUGAR
1 TEASPOON CARAWAY SEEDS
2 TEASPOONS ICING SUGAR

1 · Grease and base-line a 7 in. round cake tin with greased greaseproof paper.

2 · Sift the flour, salt and nutmeg together, and stir in the caraway seeds.

3 · Cream the butter and sugar until light and fluffy and beat in the egg yolks one at a time with a little of the flour mixture.

4 · Stir in the peel and remaining flour.

5 · Whisk the egg whites to soft peaks and fold into the cake mixture.

6 · Stir in the brandy.

7 · Put the mixture into the cake tin and sprinkle with a mixture of caster sugar and caraway seeds.

8 · Bake in a moderate oven (350°F/180°C/Gas Mark 4) for 1¼ hours.

9 · Leave in the tin for 10 minutes. Turn on to a wire rack to cool, and when cold sprinkle with sieved icing sugar.

Joan's Christmas Cake.

2½ lbs Raisins/Sultana's
6 ozs Peel.
4 ozs Cherries.
" " Gr- Almonds.
10 ozs Margarine.
10 " Sugar.
8 Eggs.
12 ozs Flour.
Pinch Salt.
2 Teasp. Mixed Spice.
1 " Nutmeg
1 Lemon Juice of & Rind.
1 Cooking Apple grated.

Rx
Cream Butter & Sugar.
Add some Egg & Flour
& Mix in grad. Add Fruit
Leave overnight to firm up.

Mix 1 Teaspoon Baking powder
just before putting in Tin.

8" 9" Square.

Porter Cake.

lb. Flour.
lb. Marg/Butter
lb. Sugar Brown.
lb. Sultanas
cup. of Stout
Teaspoon Baking Powder.
ozs Chopped Peel.
Teaspoon Nutmeg
2 " Mixed Spice.

Bake 1½ hrs in Moderate Oven.

Cheese Cake

1 lb of Cheese Cottage/Cream Cheese.
1 Pkt Pineapple Jelly
melt in ⅓ pt. of liquid.
½ Pint Cream
1 Tin Pineapple.

Base 10 ozs Crushed Goldgrain Biscuits
          3 ozs Melted Butter.

Any fruit can be used but use
appropriate Jelly flavour. Puree fruit.
If using Pineapple becomes stringy in blender
so just chop finely & mix thro' briefly in Blender
or mixer.

Rx Crush Biscuits. Mix in Melted
Butter. Put in base & chill.
Put cheese into Blender & add Cream
chop Pineapple finely — then add
Melt Jelly. If using tinned fruit,
use fruit juice & make up to ⅓
Allow to cool. Mix thro' cheese
& cream mixture. Keep some
pieces of fruit for Decoration
N.B. If using cottage cheese Blend
it before adding cream. Whip Cream
if liked & add well blended cheese
to mixer + Fruit.

RAISIN & CARROT CAKE

175 Grms Flour (Wholemeal or White) sifted
2 Teaspoons Baking Powder
1   "   Ground Cinnamon
Pinch of Mace
  "   "   Salt
2 Heaped Tablespoons seedless Raisins
100 Grms Grated Carrot
Grated Rind of ½ an Orange.
2 Tablespoons Orange Juice.
100 Grms Butter
150 Grms Brown Sugar
2 Eggs.

Sift Flour c̄ the B. Powder Salt
Mace & Cinnamon & Reserve
Mix Raisins, carrots Orange
Rind & Juice. In another bowl
cream Butter & Sugar & add
Eggs 1 at a time with a wooden
Spoon. Finally combine
c̄ the flour & carrot mixture
mix all together very well
Bake in a greased & lined
20 cm (8 inch) Tin for 40 —
minutes at 180°C 350°F
Gas Mark 4. After Removing
from the oven leave in the
Tin for 15 minutes to cool
before taking out.

The Larder

Bramble Jelly

4 lb BLACKBERRIES (SLIGHTLY UNDER-RIPE)
JUICE OF 2 LEMONS
½ PINT WATER
SUGAR

1 · Wash the fruit well and put into a pan with the lemon juice and water.
2 · Simmer for 1 hour until it is very soft.
3 · Strain through a jelly bag and measure the juice. Allow 1 lb sugar to each pint of liquid.

4 · Heat them together gently until the sugar has dissolved.
5 · Boil hard to setting point, pour into small hot jars and cover.

For a very special flavour, ¼ teaspoon each of ground nutmeg, cinnamon and mace may be stirred in just before pouring the jelly into jars.

Marrow Ginger

6 lb PREPARED MARROW
4 LEMONS
3 oz ROOT GINGER
6 lb SUGAR

1 · To prepare the marrow, peel it and discard the seeds and fibrous centre.
2 · Weigh, and then cut the marrow flesh into 1 in. cubes.
3 · Steam until just tender.
4 · Put into a bowl with the grated rind and juice of the lemons.
5 · Tie the ginger into a piece of muslin and crush with a hammer or heavy weight.

Put the ginger in the muslin into the bowl with the marrow.
6 · Add the sugar.
7 · Leave in a cool place for 24 hours.
8 · Put the mixture into a pan and stir well. Heat gently until the sugar has dissolved. Simmer until the marrow cubes are transparent and the syrup is thick.
9 · Pour into small hot jars and cover.

Cherry Chutney

3 lb BLACK CHERRIES
8 oz SEEDLESS RAISINS
4 oz DARK SOFT BROWN SUGAR
2 oz HONEY
½ PINT CIDER VINEGAR
2 TEASPOONS GROUND MIXED SPICE

1 · Chop the cherries roughly, saving all the juice which runs out. Discard the stones.
2 · Put the cherries and juice, raisins, sugar, honey, vinegar and spices into a pan. Heat gently, stirring until all the sugar has dissolved.

3 · Bring to the boil and boil for 5 minutes.
4 · Lower the heat and simmer for 30 minutes, stirring frequently.
5 · Put into small hot jars and cover with vinegar-proof lids.

This is particularly delicious with chicken or duck.

Mulled Pears

6 lb COOKING PEARS
1 lb SUGAR
1 BOTTLE RED WINE
RIND OF ½ ORANGE
RIND OF ½ LEMON
2 in. STICK CINNAMON
3 CLOVES
PINCH OF GROUND NUTMEG
WATER

1 · Use small pears which are hard and unblemished. Peel them thinly, but leave them whole with the stalks on.
2 · Pack into two or three preserving jars and sprinkle with the sugar.
3 · Divide the wine between the jars.
4 · Peel the orange and lemon rinds thinly from the fruit and divide the pieces between the jars.

5 · Add the spices and top up with water.
6 · Put on the tops and stand the jars in a very low oven (250°F/130°C/Gas Mark ½). Leave for 3 hours.
7 · Remove from the oven and screw on the tops tightly. Store in a cool dry place.
8 · Serve cold with cream.

Wines, Beers and Cordials

✗

Cherry Brandy

2 lb MORELLO CHERRIES
4 CLOVES
6 oz SUGAR
1½ PINTS BRANDY

1 · Wash and dry the cherries and remove the stones from half of them.
2 · Crack these stones and then remove the kernels.
3 · Pack the cherries into screw-top jars with kernels, cloves and sugar, and cover with brandy.
4 · Seal tightly and leave for 12 weeks, shaking the jar each week.
5 · Filter into bottles, seal and label.

Morello cherries are the deep-red, sour, cooking cherries which have a unique flavour; ordinary eating cherries are not suitable for this recipe.

Nettle Beer

2 lb YOUNG NETTLE TOPS
8 PINTS WATER
8 oz GRANULATED SUGAR
¼ oz FRESH YEAST
SMALL PIECE OF TOAST
¼ oz GROUND GINGER

1 · Boil the nettle tops in the water for 30 minutes.
2 · Strain and stir in the sugar until dissolved. Pour into a strong jar which can be corked. Spread the yeast on the toast and float it on the surface of the liquid.
3 · Add the ginger.
4 · Cover and leave to stand for 3 days.
5 · Strain into screw-top beer or cider bottles. The beer will be ready to use after 48 hours.

Spiced Red Wine

Heat a bottle of red wine, which may be home-made, with 3 tablespoons honey and ½ pint boiling water. Take an orange and stick 12 cloves into the skin. Add to the pan with a cinnamon stick and bring to the boil, but do not boil. Stir in 3 tablespoons brandy and serve at once.

Lemon Barley Water

4 oz PEARL BARLEY
2 LEMONS
2 oz CUBE SUGAR
2 PINTS BOILING WATER

1 · Wash the barley and put into a saucepan.

2 · Just cover with cold water and bring to the boil.

3 · Boil for 4 minutes and strain off the water.

4 · Put the barley into a large jug.

5 · Rub the yellow zest off the lemons with the cube sugar and put into the jug.

6 · Pour in the boiling water and stir to dissolve the sugar. Leave until cold.

7 · Squeeze the juice out of the lemons and stir into the jug.

8 · Strain before serving, diluting to taste.

Sweetmeats

Plain Toffee

8 fl oz WATER
1 lb DEMERARA SUGAR
8 oz BUTTER
2 TEASPOONS LEMON JUICE

1 · Heat the water and sugar gently until the sugar has dissolved.

2 · Boil to hard crack stage (i.e. when a little of the mixture dropped in cold water separates into threads which are hard and brittle – temperature 310°F/154°C).

3 · Stir in the butter and lemon juice and beat until melted.

4 · Pour into a greased tin and mark into squares when cool.

5 · Leave the toffee until cold before breaking it into pieces.

Candied Chestnuts

2 lb CHESTNUTS
2 lb CASTER SUGAR
2 PINTS WATER
1 CINNAMON STICK
1 VANILLA POD

1 · Score the chestnut shells with a sharp knife.

2 · Cover with cold water and bring to the boil.

3 · Simmer for 30 minutes.

4 · Cool slightly and remove the shells and inner skins.

5 · Put into a large bowl. Put the sugar, water, cinnamon and vanilla pod into a thick pan and heat gently until the sugar has dissolved.

6 · Pour over the chestnuts and cover with a clean cloth. Leave overnight.

7 · Drain off the syrup and bring to the boil.

8 · Remove the cinnamon stick and vanilla pod.

9 · Pour the syrup over the chestnuts and leave to stand for 6 hours.

10 · Put the syrup and chestnuts into a preserving pan and heat gently. Simmer for 2 hours without boiling.

11 · Remove the chestnuts with a slotted spoon and place them in jars.

12 · Boil the syrup until it is as thick as warm golden syrup.

13 · Pour over the chestnuts, cool and seal tightly.

14 · Leave in the jars for 4 weeks.

15 · Drain the chestnuts and boil the syrup.

16 · Add the chestnuts and take off the heat. Leave to stand for 20 minutes.

17 · Drain the chestnuts and put on a wire rack to drain completely.

18 · Store in an airtight box, or wrap individual chestnuts in foil.

Sugar Mice

2 lb GRANULATED SUGAR
¼ PINT WATER
3 oz POWDERED GLUCOSE
FEW DROPS OF PINK COLOURING
THIN WHITE STRING

1 · Put the sugar and water into a pan and heat gently until the sugar has dissolved.
2 · Add the glucose and boil to soft ball stage (i.e. when a little of the mixture dropped in cold water can be formed into a soft ball when rolled in the fingers – temperature 237°F/114°C).
3 · Cool without stirring until the mixture thickens.
4 · Pour on to a wet surface and work in the pink colouring with a spatula until the mixture is firm and opaque and the colour is even (some of the mixture may be left uncoloured, but must still be worked until opaque).
5 · Divide into 16 pieces, and shape into fat mice, moulding the ears carefully.
6 · Mark the eyes with a matchstick, or insert silver cake balls.
7 · Cut string into 3 in. lengths, and press into the mice for tails.
8 · Leave until dry.

Peppermint Humbugs

1 lb DEMERARA SUGAR
¼ PINT WATER
2 oz BUTTER
3 DROPS OIL OF PEPPERMINT
PINCH OF CREAM OF TARTAR

1 · Put the sugar, water, butter, oil of peppermint and cream of tartar into a heavy saucepan.
2 · Heat gently until the sugar has dissolved, and then boil to soft crack stage (i.e. when a little of the mixture dropped in cold water separates into threads which are hard but not brittle – temperature 280°F/140°C).
3 · Take off the heat and cool for about 2 minutes.
4 · Pour on to an oiled slab or tin.
5 · When the mixture is cool enough to handle, pull into long strips. Divide the mixture in half, and pull half until it becomes paler than the other half. Twist the two halves together and cut into short pieces, or "cushions".

Coconut Ice

1 lb GRANULATED SUGAR
¼ PINT MILK
4 oz DESICCATED COCONUT
FEW DROPS OF PINK COLOURING

1 · Grease a shallow tin lightly.

2 · Put the sugar and milk into a heavy saucepan and heat gently until the mixture boils, stirring all the time with a wooden spoon.

3 · Boil gently to soft ball stage (i.e. when a little of the mixture dropped in cold water can be formed into a soft ball when rolled in the fingers – temperature 237°F/114°C).

4 · Take off the heat and beat in the coconut quickly.

5 · Pour half the mixture into the tin and spread it evenly.

6 · Add a few drops of the pink colouring to the remaining mixture, and pour on top of the white coconut ice.

7 · When cold and firm, cut the Coconut Ice into squares or bars.

Home and Beauty

Cucumber Face Wash

2 CUCUMBERS
EAU DE COLOGNE

1 · Wipe the cucumbers but do not peel them.

2 · Cut into small pieces and blend in a liquidiser or food processor, or mash with a potato masher.

3 · Put into a pan and simmer for 10 minutes.

4 · Strain off the liquid and measure.

5 · Add 1 tablespoon eau de cologne to each pint of liquid, and then bottle it.

6 · Sponge the face with this liquid two or three times a day.

Freckle Cleanser

Warm some clear honey and add enough crushed fennel seeds to make a thick mixture. Spread on the face and leave for 15 minutes. Wash off with warm water.

Hand Cream

4 oz LARD
2 EGG YOLKS
1 TABLESPOON CLEAR HONEY
1 TABLESPOON ROSEWATER
5 DROPS ALMOND ESSENCE

Soften the lard and work in the other ingredients. Put into a screw-top jar and keep by the sink. The cream softens the hands, but also helps to heal minor cracks and scratches.

Sweet Bags

These little bags full of mixed herbs and spices give a subtle scent to cupboards and drawers. Make them from small pieces of pretty fabric trimmed with ribbon or odd bits of lace. Dry equal quantities of rosemary, thyme and bay leaves and then rub them into very small pieces. Put into the small bags and sew up firmly.

For a variation, use a mixture of 2 parts mint, 2 parts rosemary, 1 part thyme and 1 part ground cloves. A light fragrance may be obtained by mixing 1 tablespoon lavender flowers, 1 tablespoon rosemary and 1 tablespoon thyme with 1 teaspoon pennyroyal, 1 teaspoon ground cloves and 1 teaspoon dried lemon peel.

Onion Cleansers

The juice of a raw onion removes rust stains on steel – just rub over the stains with a halved onion and then polish. Onion juice also polishes tinware which should be rubbed with a slice and the juice left to dry on the metal before polishing in the usual way.

Burnt food on an aluminium saucepan may be removed if an onion is rubbed well into the area and the pan is then filled with water and boiled briskly for 30 minutes. The burnt food will be loosened and the pan will be clean.

If cotton or linen is scorched during ironing, rub the area with slices of raw onion, letting the juice soak in for 10 minutes. Wash in warm soapy water and rinse in tepid water.

Remedies

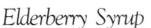

Elderberry Syrup

2 lb RIPE ELDERBERRIES
2 PINTS WATER
1 oz ROOT GINGER
6 CLOVES
SUGAR
4 TABLESPOONS GIN OR BRANDY

1 · Put the berries into a pan with water, crushed ginger and cloves.
2 · Simmer for 30 minutes.
3 · Strain, pressing out all the juice.
4 · Measure the liquid and allow 8 oz sugar to each pint liquid.
5 · Stir over low heat until the sugar dissolves.
6 · Boil for 10 minutes.
7 · Remove from the heat, cool and stir in gin or brandy.
8 · Pour into small screw-top jars or small bottles.
9 · Store in the refrigerator.

Use a little in cold water for a summer drink, or add boiling water for a winter cold. Elderberry syrup in hot water is very soothing for a sore throat or cough.

Blackcurrant Mint Tea

4 oz DRIED BLACKCURRANT LEAVES
2 oz DRIED MINT
2 oz CHINESE GREEN TEA

1 · Pick the blackcurrant leaves when they are young and tender just when the fruit is beginning to form (early May is the usual time).
2 · Dry the leaves in a warm place and crumble them, along with the mint. Mix with the tea and put into an airtight tin.
3 · Use 2 tablespoons of this tea to a small teapot of boiling water.
This tea has a delicious flavour and is very soothing. It makes a good digestive drink after a meal.

Rheumatism Reliever

Boil 1 oz celery seed in 1 pint water until the liquid is reduced by half. Strain and bottle. Take 1 teaspoon of the mixture in a little water twice a day for 14 days.

Lime Tea

Gather lime flowers from the trees in July on a dry day. Spread them out on paper in a warm room or leave them in the sun for 2-3 days to dry. Store in an airtight box or jar where they will keep for about 9 months. Use a small handful of dried lime flowers for each person with a cupful of boiling water. Leave to stand for 2-3 minutes, strain and sweeten with honey or sugar to taste. This tea is very soothing and is a remedy against sleeplessness.

Treacle Posset

A favourite drink for soothing the digestion and inducing sleep. For 1 person, heat ½ pint milk with 1 tablespoon black treacle until almost boiling. Pour into a mug and float 2 teaspoons double cream on top. Sprinkle with ground nutmeg or cinnamon and serve at once.

Memory Strengthener

Infuse 1 oz lemon balm in 1 pint boiling water for 15 minutes. Strain and bottle. Drink often with the addition of a little lemon juice and sugar.

Miscellaneous

Mushroom Ketchup

2 lb MUSHROOMS
3 oz COOKING SALT
1 PINT VINEGAR
1 TEASPOON ALLSPICE BERRIES
1 TEASPOON BLACK PEPPERCORNS
6 BLADES MACE
4 CLOVES
1 SMALL PIECE ROOT GINGER
1 in. CINNAMON STICK

1 · Trim the ends of the mushroom stalks. Wipe the mushrooms but do not wash or peel them. Break the mushroom caps and stalks into small pieces and arrange in layers with salt in a bowl.

2 · Cover with a cloth and leave to stand in a cool place for 5 days, stirring once or twice a day and pressing out mushroom juices.

3 · Cover with foil and bake in a low oven (300°F/150°C/Gas Mark 2) for 1½ hours.

4 · Strain through a jelly bag or clean tea-cloth for an hour until all the liquid has dripped through.

5 · Put the liquid into a pan with the vinegar and crushed spices.

6 · Simmer gently until the liquid has been reduced to half. Strain through muslin into a clean saucepan.

7 · Bring to the boil and pour into clean hot sauce bottles with screw-tops.

8 · Screw on tops tightly and then release one half-turn.

9 · Put the bottles into a large pan on a rack and cover with hot but not boiling water.

10 · Bring the temperature to 150°F/54°C. Keep the water at this temperature for 30 minutes.

11 · Remove bottles and screw on tops tightly.

12 · Store in a cool place.

13 · Use a few drops of the ketchup to flavour soups, stews and sauces.

Buttered Rum

For each person, heat a china mug and put in 1 teaspoon light soft brown sugar. Add 4 tablespoons boiling water, 4 tablespoons rum and a nut of butter. Stir well and sprinkle with ground nutmeg.

Nursery Butter

REDCURRANTS
BLACKCURRANTS
GOOSEBERRIES
STRAWBERRIES
SUGAR

This is a lovely way of using up all the oddments of soft fruit at the end of the season, and the proportions of the different fruit don't matter much. For each 2 lb fruit, allow 1 lb sugar.

1 · Remove the currant stems.

2 · Top and tail the gooseberries and hull the strawberries.

3 · Mix the fruit in a preserving pan and heat gently until the juices are running freely.

4 · Stir in the sugar over low heat and then boil until very thick.

5 · Pour into small hot jars and cover.

Cinnamon Sugar

1 lb CASTER SUGAR
4 CINNAMON STICKS

1 · Put the sugar into a jar and push in the cinnamon sticks.

2 · Seal tightly.

3 · Use the cinnamon-flavoured sugar for cakes, biscuits and puddings.

4 · For concentrated flavour, mix caster sugar and ground cinnamon, allowing 1 teaspoon spice to 2 oz sugar.

5 · Stir together until evenly coloured and store in a screw-top jar.

6 · Use in fruit cakes and gingerbreads, and to make cinnamon toast (just sprinkle the flavoured sugar on to buttered toast).

Mock Capers

1½ lb NASTURTIUM SEEDS
2 PINTS VINEGAR
2 oz COOKING SALT
12 PEPPERCORNS
2 CLOVES
4 TARRAGON LEAVES

1 · Try to choose even-sized small nasturtium seeds. Wash them well and put into a bowl. Cover with cold water and leave to stand overnight.

2 · Mix the vinegar with salt, peppercorns, cloves and tarragon and also leave to stand overnight.

3 · Drain the seeds and put into small screw-topped jars with vinegar-proof lids. Cover with vinegar, dividing the peppercorns and tarragon leaves between the jars.

4 · Cover tightly and try to keep for 1 year before using.